IMAGES
of America

WEST CHESTER

WEST-CHESTER GAZETTE.

PUBLISHED on every WEDNESDAY by JONES, HOPP & DERRICK, opposite the Court House, West-Chester.

Vol. I.—No. 1. WEDNESDAY, January 2, 1793. Price Two Dollars per Annum.

INTRODUCTION.

WITH deference to the Public, the Editor thinks it needless to make any voluntary remarks, on offering the first number of the West-Chester Gazette.

The present public spirit manifested in their consideration to recommend an impartial conveyance of News and Politics in opposition to Folly, and a faithful herald of State and of Government transactions.

The latter being of the utmost importance to the public, a considerable part of this paper will be appropriated for that purpose.

Improvements relative to Agriculture...

Political controversies will meet with...

Communications from Literary characters...

The West-Chester Gazette is now submitted to the Public...

THE EDITOR.

January 1st, 1793.

THE HIVE.

On Sentiment.

ALL beneficence flows from the act of a way of feeling...

Remarks on the Death of Louis XVI. with a sketch of his character.

[By the Marquis of Lansdown.]

MY present consideration...

American Intelligence.

PHILADELPHIA, Jan. 3d, 1794.

Extract of a letter from Baltimore.

"An American vessel is just arrived from Havre de Grace..."

BOSTON, Dec. 15.

THE PROSPECT OF PEACE.

IMAGES
of America

WEST CHESTER

Martha Carson-Gentry and Paul Rodebaugh

ARCADIA

First published 1997
Copyright © Martha Carson-Gentry and Paul Rodebaugh, 1997

ISBN 0-7524-0871-2

Published by Arcadia Publishing,
an imprint of the Chalford Publishing Corporation,
One Washington Center, Dover, New Hampshire 03820.
Printed in Great Britain

Library of Congress Cataloging-in-Publication Data applied for

To Bonnie Bailey Carson, better known as Mama,
and Leslee and Allison

To Mother,
Madeleine W. Rodebaugh

Contents

About the Photographs

Many amateur and professional photographers produced the photographs used in this work. Among the most interesting are four men who worked in the borough from 1880–1940. The two earliest were Gilbert Cope and Charles S. Bradford. Albert Biles and Joseph Belt worked mainly from 1895 to 1940.

Charles S. Bradford was an amateur photographer who also practiced law in West Chester. He lived on Dean Street between Church and Darlington Streets. His father, James Bradford, was listed in the Directory of West Chester in 1857. Four early photographs of C.S. Bradford are included in this book.

Gilbert Cope (1840–1928) lived in West Chester for nearly forty years and took many of the glass-plate negatives which we have used. Cope was a historian and had an eye for the significant which he used to record West Chester in the 1880s and '90s.

Albert Biles began working in the borough in the last decade of the nineteenth century. He was the photographer for the Centennial Booklet produced in 1899. He worked in the borough at various locations until 1942.

Joseph Belt began his work as a professional photographer in West Chester shortly after the turn of the century. He was also an inventor of note. One of his inventions shot a baseball out of the Chester County Court House at noon during the summertime to a waiting crowd of young boys. A second invention was a clock which would regulate the heating of the house by turning off and on the furnace at a given time of the day. There are several of his photographs throughout the book.

Introduction

In two years the Borough of West Chester will celebrate the bicentennial of its founding in 1799. Three hundred years ago the location of West Chester was yet to be surveyed and was the edge of the settlement of colonial Pennsylvania. Nathaniel Puckle, a ships captain who had received a grant from William Penn in 1701, and the Haines family of Evesham, New Jersey, purchased a large grant in this area about the same time. These two farms took up about three quarters of the land in the present borough.

Native Americans had camped within the limits of the borders of the borough in times past and the remains of eight campsites have been located. By 1760 four farms met at a crossroads of the road from Pottstown to Wilmington and the road from Philadelphia to the Brandywine Creek, the present High and Gay Streets. When the American Revolution came to Chester County at the time of the Battle of Brandywine on September 11, 1777, a few buildings, mostly farmhouses, a log schoolhouse, and a log tavern known as the Turk's Head had been built near this intersection. This area, then a part of Goshen Township in Chester County, had no name and the local residents, when asked their location, would say that they lived near the Turk's Head Tavern in Goshen.

After the battle the British army passed through the village on their way to the Chester Valley. The log schoolhouse served as a hospital where British and American wounded were treated. The soldiers who died were buried in the garden of the old tavern.

The county seat was moved from Chester to West Chester in 1786 and the town began to grow. John Hannum, the Father of West Chester, bought the Hoopes farm to the northwest of the crossroads and before 1795 sold building lots along the present Gay Street. The other farms were laid out as building lots and the original streets—Church, High, Gay, Market, Chestnut, and Walnut—were established.

During the first quarter of the nineteenth century the West Chester Academy and several other private schools were opened and West Chester became known as an educational center.

West Chester was fortunate because accomplished architects were selected to design churches, residences, and public buildings. William Strickland, Thomas U. Walter, Samuel Sloan, Addison Hutton, Frank Furness, and T. Roney Williamson contributed to the enrichment of the architectural heritage in the nineteenth century. Because of the many private schools and the fine examples of Greek Revival architecture the town became known as the "Athens of Pennsylvania."

Although West Chester never attracted heavy industry the production of wagon wheels and the Sharples Cream Separator became known throughout the world. The West Chester State Normal School, a teacher training institution, was established in the borough in 1871 and has grown into the West Chester University of Pennsylvania.

The location of West Chester on a height of land between the watersheds of the Brandywine and Chester Creeks has been known for its healthy environment. Over the past two centuries the open land within the original borough limits has been developed into housing and some of the old industrial plants have been converted into apartments.

The population of West Chester in 1800 was 374. By 1900 the population had grown to 4,757 and by 1970 approximately 19,000 people resided here. The downtown area is now a historical district containing many interesting buildings dating to the early nineteenth century.

Martha Carson-Gentry and Paul Rodebaugh
West Chester, Pennsylvania
May 28, 1997

One

Front Porches
and Chimneys

Jerome Gray and his family sit on their front porch on the southwest corner of Church and Lafayette Streets. The home, designed by T. Roney Williamson, was built in 1881. Jerome's son, Norman D. Gray, who also lived in this house, was the state librarian of Pennsylvania. Church Street is one of the original streets in the borough. The name came from the church built by the Baptists on the west side of this street, half of a block south of Market Street.

Fountain Green is the longest continuously occupied house in West Chester. It was built by Samuel Hoopes Jr. in 1773 and is located at 200 N. Church Street. John Hannum, founder of West Chester, lived here as did John Rutter, a Philadelphia lawyer. Rutter owned the home for over thirty years and moved it from the center of Church Street in 1857. T. Roney Williamson, an architect who designed many homes in West Chester, also lived here.

This interesting stone house was built in 1886 on the southwest corner of Biddle and Church Streets. The house was unusual because it was built of uncut boulders and bricks. It was razed in the 1960s for a parking lot. Town houses have since been built on the property.

This house at 429 N. Church Street dates back to the 1850s. The William P. Townsend family lived here at the turn of the century. It was later known as the Bailey House. It currently is the home of Martha Carson-Gentry, co-author of this book, her mother, Bonnie Bailey Carson, and Martha's bull terrier, Nadine.

T. Roney Williamson designed this stone mansion for attorney William M. Hayes and his wife, Rachel Russell Hayes, on the southwest corner of Church and Marshall Streets. Their son, John Russell Hayes, known as the "Quaker Poet" grew up here. His first book of verse was published in 1895.

This Queen Anne-style house at 523 N.Church Street was the home of historian Gilbert Cope, a noted genealogist and photographer. Cope took a number of the pictures used in this book. He was the co-author with J. Smith Futhey of *The History of Chester County*.

The Stephen Paxson Darlington "cottage," built in 1881, was also designed by T. Roney Williamson. The estate took up one square block, bounded by Church, Virginia, High, and Ashbridge Streets. This is a wonderful example of the Queen Anne style that was popular in the late nineteenth century. Darlington was one of the founders of the Hoopes Bros. and Darlington Wheel Works.

The Joshua Hoopes Boarding School, built in 1836 on the southeast corner of Biddle and Matlack Streets, is shown here as it appeared c. 1900. Hoopes, a noted naturalist in the area, was one of the three men who laid out Marshall Square Park. The familiar brick wall which now surrounds this home was added during the 1920s.

The Barclay Home, operated by the Society of Friends, originally occupied this building, located next to their meetinghouse at the northeast corner of Church and Chestnut Streets. The Barclay provided a permanent place for aged or infirm Friends or Friendly People. The Samuel M. Painter House is just east of the Barclay. The Painter House was one of the few stations on the Underground Railroad in the borough of West Chester.

The Sharples Homestead at 22 Dean Street was in the same family for 240 years. Eight generations of the Sharples family have resided here. The original house, built of logs prior to 1750, was located just southwest of the present house and was removed in 1802. The original section of this house was built near that time. The barn in the picture was moved in 1838 to a

location along Price Street, where it was destroyed by lightning before the Civil War. Martha Sharples drew this pen-and-ink sketch showing her family home, which was at one time a 203.5-acre farmstead extending across the borough from east to west. The Lombardy Poplars were typical of West Chester in this early period.

This house on the northwest corner of Barnard and Walnut Streets looks quite different today. It is now painted yellow and is surrounded by a brick wall. Barnard Street was named by William Everhart in honor of Isaac D. Barnard. Barnard was a major in the War of 1812, a lawyer, the attorney general for Chester County, a state senator, the secretary of Pennsylvania, and a U.S. senator. He died at the age of forty-three in 1834.

The large brick house located at 325–327 S. High Street was the Yarnall-Webb home. It is presently offices and apartments, but it has changed very little in appearance.

This house at 408 S. Walnut Street was occupied from 1938 until 1980 by Dr. Arthur James. Dr. James wrote definitive histories of the potters and clockmakers in Chester County. His pioneer work *Chester County Clocks and their Makers* was published in 1947. He also wrote a volume on the numerous covered bridges in Chester County.

Anne Y. Stone stands in front of her home on the northeast corner of Market and Walnut Street, about 1910. Anne Y. Stone was the last surviving founding member of the Westminster Presbyterian Church. The Salvation Army Headquarters is located on this corner today.

This Victorian home at 221 W. Miner Street was the residence of John A. Rupert. Rupert was a money lender and conveyancer. Edward Savery lived in the left-hand side at 223. Miner Street was named for a distinguished citizen of the borough, Charles Miner, editor of *The Village Record* newspaper.

This night-blooming Cereus, or the Queen of the Night, was a very popular plant in West Chester. The blooms of this succulent come out of the leaves and last for only one night. Many families in the borough held night-blooming Cereus parties and invited friends and neighbors to see this spectacular show of nature.

The home of Howard and Elizabeth Heston at 309 N. Matlack Street is shown here after a major blizzard. This picture was taken from the yard of the Hannum house at the corner of Biddle and Matlack. The riders were probably breaking a path in the street so it would be passable. The street was known as Matlack Street because Robert Matlack had at one time owned the land.

The Craven Mansion on the northwest corner of Matlack and Biddle Streets was erected *c.* 1890. John V. Craven, a novelist who wrote *The Leaf is Green* and *Waterfront Mark*, was born in this house.

This Victorian home on the northeast corner of Biddle and Walnut Streets was built in two sections. The left section, with the quoins, is the original structure with the addition on the right added shortly after the first section was completed.

This house, across from Marshall Square Park on the southwest corner of Biddle and Franklin Streets, was built c. 1900. It remains a private residence.

Wilmer Woodward took this photo postcard of 313 West Biddle Street about 1910. He and his family lived in the right side of this home for over forty years. Mr. Woodward was the grandfather of Paul Rodebaugh, co-author of this book.

T. Lawrence Eyre, a state senator from the West Chester district, built this house, Eyreview, shortly after the turn of the century. T. Lawrence Eyre was a local benefactor who gave a yearly Christmas party for children at the Brinton's Feed Store on N. Church Street. The building on the left was the four-car garage, which sported chauffeur quarters on the second floor.

Daniel and Alice Hoopes received 220 acres in 1730 and built the earliest home in the northwest quadrant of West Chester in 1736. The house on Biddle Street was located on the present site of the Elks Club. The date stone was removed when the old house was torn down about 1880. It was preserved in the kitchen of the old mansion, now a part of the Elks Club.

Among the earliest structures in West Chester was the Turk's Head Tavern. The crossroads was the center of the village at the time of the Revolution. Joseph Hoopes built the tavern in 1769, as evidenced by the date stone. The brick tavern became the core of a small number of dwellings located near the Philadelphia and Wilmington Roads.

Two

Along the Brick Sidewalks

A blizzard crippled West Chester in February of 1899. The parishioners of St. Agnes Church on Gay Street can be seen clearing the property. In the center of the picture is Academy Row erected on the grounds of the former West Chester Academy, the forerunner of West Chester University.

This Samuel J. Parker postcard is of the corner of High and Gay Streets about 1908. A.C. Whitcraft's shoe store is on the left corner and Fred Wahl's hat shop is on the right as you look west on Gay Street. High Street was so named because it follows the height of land between the Brandywine and Chester Creeks. No one seems to know exactly how Gay Street got its name.

The Borough Council passed an ordinance in 1848 to establish a park in the northeastern section of West Chester. Marshall Square Park contains approximately 5.5 acres. It was named in honor of Humphrey Marshall, the noted botanist who had written the first book describing the native forest trees. The park contained 200 ornamental trees and shrubs representing about 160 varieties.

The 97th Regiment of the Pa. Volunteer Infantry erected this monument in 1887 at the highest point in the borough. Men were recruited for the 97th in 1861 and served until August 26, 1865. Henry R. Guss was the commanding officer. The monument was built on the former site of the borough reservoir. Memorial Day services have been held here for over a century.

The Farmers and Mechanics Trust Company erected this skyscraper, one of two in the suburbs of Philadelphia, in 1907. Unfortunately, this bank failed during the Depression. At one time The Overtown Restaurant was operated on the roof of the building.

The new post office was in the process of being built on the northeast corner of Walnut and Gay Streets in December 1905. The building was built of stone from the Avondale Quarries. Smith's Funeral Home in the background was in business here for over 115 years.

The Everhart Block is shown at the northwest corner of Market and Church Streets. William Everhart, who developed the Wollerton tract south of Market Street, built this building as his general store before the middle of the nineteenth century. This was an important business beginning in the 1840s.

This view of Market Street looking east from Church was taken shortly before the turn of the century. The trolley tracks on Market Street terminated at the railroad station four blocks east down the street.

Thomas Hogue's store is one of the few building in central West Chester made with local serpentine or green stone. The Hogue store sold general merchandise, many examples of which are displayed on the brick sidewalk.

27

T. Walter Hannum (center) and two of his friends sit on the curb of the brick sidewalk in front of the Hannum house on N. Matlack Street. Hannum served as president of the Class of 1912 at West Chester High School. Several of the pictures in this book belong to his daughter, Caroline Rubincam.

At the turn of the century the Darlington Brothers grocery store was on the right looking north on Church Street from Market. This wholesale and retail business specialized in fancy groceries, staples, and novelties. They advertised "Three Seal" brand flour, Strode's sausage and scrapple, foreign cheese, and olive oil in the local paper.

Joseph Belt, a local photographer, took this picture of the ice storm at the Ralston Hoopes home at the northeast corner of Union and Walnut Streets, February 22, 1902. Belt published a series of pictures documenting this storm

This was a familiar scene in the area prior to the age of the automobile. This horse and buggy were waiting in front of a home on N. Church Street on June 28, 1899.

The Lenape trolley, passing the Everhart Fountain at W. Market Street at Church, on a summer evening, has been captured by this early postcard.

The Green Tree Inn, which was replaced by the Green Tree Building in 1929, was operated by Henry Ruhl Guss during the Civil War. Guss served as a colonel of the 97th Regiment Pennsylvania Volunteer Infantry which he raised from local residents. At the turn of the twentieth century the owner of the Green Tree Inn was Benjamin Vendever.

The carbarn of the West Chester Street Railway Company is on the left next to The Daily Local News office, c. 1915. The first issue of *The Daily Local News* was published on Tuesday afternoon, November 19, 1872. The first two issues were free and on the third day regular carriers were put on the street to sell subscriptions.

On June 14, 1872, a formal Library Committee was appointed to found a public library. In 1886 Hannah M. Darlington gave a plot of land at the corner of Church and Lafayette Streets for a library building, which was designed by T. Roney Williamson and opened in 1888. Lafayette Street was named after General Lafayette, who aided the Americans in the Revolutionary war. He re-visited West Chester on July 26, 1825, reviewed the troops who paraded in his honor, and gave a speech at the courthouse.

Winters in West Chester are often quite beautiful. Though snow storms are more common an occasional ice storm can wreak havoc in a very short period of time. The above picture shows a snow storm at Walnut and Union Streets. The picture below, taken by Joseph Belt looking south from Virginia Avenue onto Church Street, shows the destruction caused by the ice storm of February 22, 1899.

The Red Arrow line car which is about to return to Philadelphia awaits passengers in front of the Green Tree Inn on Gay Street at High.

The Chester County Hospital, established in 1892, was originally located between Matlack and Franklin Streets on Marshall Street. One of the first patients was Benjamin Bush, who had been found on the railroad under the Gay Street bridge with both legs cut off below the knee. He recovered and the reputation of the hospital grew. This 1907 postcard shows the brick buildings from Marshall Square Park. These buildings were replaced when the hospital moved to West Goshen township less than a half mile away in 1925. Anna Jarvis, the founder of Mother's Day, died in this building when it was later used as a nursing home.

Smedley Darlington Butler sits on the fence in front his childhood home on W. Miner Street, c. 1886. Referred to by his men as "Old Gimlet Eye," Butler was a Quaker marine general who won two congressional medals of honor during his service career.

WEST CHESTER IN 1842

Sherman Day made this famous wood cut looking north on High Street for his book *Historical Collections of Pennsylvania* published in 1842. This wood cut has been used as a logo for the borough and individual businesses such as Mostellers. Barclay Rubincam used it as a reference for his familiar painting of downtown West Chester.

Three

Downtown, Intown, Uptown

The railroad connecting Philadelphia to West Chester through Media was completed in 1858 and later connected to the earlier Frazer branch. This is the first train from Philadelphia arriving in West Chester in November 1858.

In the second decade of the nineteenth century a row of log houses extended north on the west side of High Street from Barnard to the Black Bear Tavern at Market Street. Gradually these structures were replaced by those of stone, some by native serpentine. This building, located on the site of the West Chester Street Railway carbarn, was the last of these log structures to survive. Olof Stromberg operated a shoemakers shop in this building from 1818 to his death in 1871.

William Everhart, a prominent merchant who developed much of the southwest quadrant of West Chester, and his family were remembered by this fountain. It was erected by his son, James Bowen Everhart, in the center of Market Street west of Church. The building housing the original Everhart Store is on the left and a West Chester Street Railway car is about to cross Church Street.

The Goodwill Fire Company No. 2 was founded in 1833. The building on the left with the bell tower was the original home of Old Number 2. The buildings in the center and on the right were razed almost fifty years ago for a parking lot for the National Bank of Chester County and Trust Company. The photograph was by C.S. Bradford, a local photographer. Goodwill is presently located on Gay Street east of High.

Fame Fire Company Number 3, once located on the first block of East Market Street, was established in 1838. The building shown in this photo postcard was demolished for the parking lot of the First National Bank of West Chester.

HOME OF "WESSIE."

This postcard was distributed at a fireman's parade in S. Bethlehem, Pennsylvania, on October 22, 1905. The picture is of West Chester Fire Company No. 1, the first fire company organized in West Chester. The first meeting was held on August 6, 1799, eleven years after the town was incorporated. There were twenty-two founding members, all of whom were prominent residents of the borough.

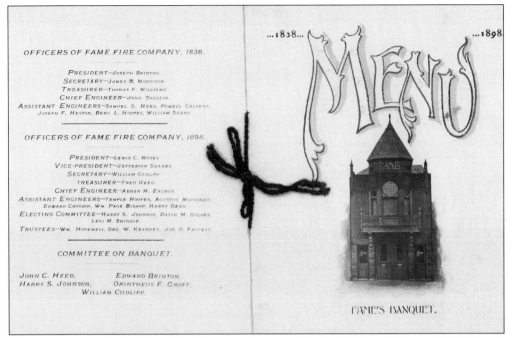

This program was for the Fame Fire Company Banquet held in 1898 to celebrate their 60th year of service to the community.

A photograph of the Good Will Drum Corps was taken on the east portico of the Chester County Court House around the turn of the century.

Members of Fame Fire Company Number 3 display their horse-drawn firefighting equipment in front of the firehouse on east Market Street, *c.* 1908.

The Joseph B. Smith Funeral Home also provided furniture and upholstering in all of its branches. The first floor in the front of the building on 17 E. Gay Street was Joseph Dick's furniture store. Shown here c. 1910, his business offered a full and complete line of furniture such as parlor and bed room suites, spring mattresses, cots, carpets, mattings, and "other things too numerous to mention."

41

The Horticultural Society building, located on N. High Street, was designed by Thomas U. Walter (1804–1887). It featured a recessed Norman arch as its focus, and was erected in 1848, making it the second building in the country built expressly for the promotion of horticulture. This hall was used for floral shows, a Women's Rights Convention in 1852, anti-slavery meetings, etc. Among the guests who appeared here were Lucretia Mott, Sojourner Truth, Elizabeth Cady Stanton, Buffalo Bill, Horace Greeley, Henry Ward Beecher, and Thomas Nast.

This building, which housed the Chester County Trust Company on East Gay Street, was built in 1905. It is currently the home of The Founder's Bank.

The Hemphill Building once stood at 9 N. High Street and was being razed when this photograph was taken in 1912.

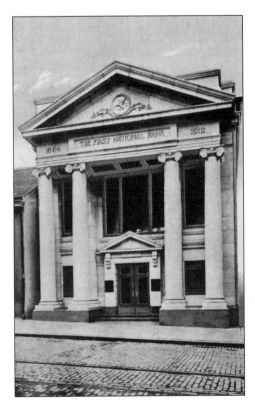

The First National Bank, constructed by Cloyd Baldwin, replaced the Hemphill Building at 9 N. High Street the same year. The bank was organized in 1863 and remains the First National Bank. George Brinton, the first president, served until January 15, 1869. Brinton was succeeded by William Wollerton, who served until his death on April 28, 1898.

The Hickman Fountain stands in front of the Chester County Courthouse on High Street. It was paid for by Mrs. John Hickman, wife of the local representative to the U.S. Congress. It was built in 1869 as a watering hole for horses, dogs, and people. The 6-foot-high marble fountain is topped by a large round ball, which disappears on occasion.

The New Century Club Fountain, located on North High Street near the borough limits, was designed in 1898 by Martha G. Cornwell, a gifted sculptor. It was used as a watering trough for horses. The trough is granite with a bronze figure of a boy kneeling with a watering bucket in his right hand. The fountain was a gift from P.M. Sharples. This bronze statue mysteriously disappeared during the blizzard of 1958. The abominable snowman was at it again.

The National Bank of Chester County was the first bank to be established in Chester County. The building was designed by Thomas U. Walter and completed in 1837. It was often called the "old white bank" because it was built of white marble. A railroad spur was constructed from the Frazer branch to the Thomas quarry in Chester Valley to bring the supply of marble needed for the bank. The entrance to the bank was lowered in 1928.

The architectural centerpiece of the borough is the Chester County Court House on the corner of High and Market Streets. It was also designed by Thomas U. Walter, the noted Greek Revival architect. It was built of brick and faced with Indiana limestone in 1846–47. The corinthian columns were made of iron and filled with cement. The total cost of construction was $55,345.98.

The West Chester Hotel at the top of Hannum Avenue hill was built by Joseph L. Taylor. Hannum Avenue had been known as Strasburg Road, which was laid out in 1794. The hotel was opened in 1828 by Jane P. Jefferis, whose husband, John, once ran the Washington Hotel adjacent to the courthouse. The hotel was torn down over thirty years ago to create a municipal parking lot. The Reilly family occupied this building as a home for many years.

The Turk's Head Tavern was the center of the colonial village and served as a meeting place for the local residents for nearly two centuries. The name Turk's Head came from the tavern sign. During the Revolution the tavern keeper was a loyalist. In the decade of the 1840s this building served as a girl's school. The building was replaced in the 1960s by the Dime Savings Bank.

The Farmer's Hotel on the north side of W. Market Street between Darlington and New Streets was popular in the late nineteenth century. During the first half of the twentieth century it was an apartment building. It was razed for a municipal parking lot approximately thirty-five years ago.

Most inns and hotels had livery stables attached to supply their patrons with transportation. The Turk's Head Tavern had a livery stable prior to the age of cars. The Turk's Head Garage replaced the livery stable in the 1920s. This structure is now part of the First National Bank.

Looking northeast from the courthouse tower the smoke stack of the West Chester Electric plant can be plainly seen. The original electric plant was destroyed by an explosion at 4:20 pm on December 16, 1887. Six local residents were killed in the tragedy.

Traffic control at the busy intersection of High and Gay Streets was quite primitive in 1910. By turning the control signal the officer directed traffic during the warmer months. In the winter he occupied a small wooden house which protected him from the elements. The traffic mechanism was on the top of the house.

Four

People at Work

People in West Chester have had outstanding careers in many fields. Included in their endeavors have been education, finance, medicine, agriculture, politics, manufacturing, religion, the arts, and law, to mention a few. Wilmer Woodward, shown here operating a lathe in the machine shop at the Sharples Separator Works, was the grandfather of Paul Rodebaugh, a co-author of this book. This image was taken in 1914 when Wilmer was the foreman of the shop.

Fred Wahl and his son owned the hat shop at the northwest corner of High and Gay Streets. This building was torn down in 1928 and replaced by the F.W. Woolworth Building.

The Ralston R. Hoopes Coal Yard was located at 209–211 S. Matlack Street. Coal was delivered in the two-wheeled carts that are on the street in front of the office. His motto stated, "Good coal is always cheap coal."

George Moses sold harnesses, blankets, and wagons of his own manufacturing at his carriage shop at 15 N. Walnut Street. The brake cart in the middle of this picture was made by Moses. He also advertised Delaval Cream Separators, an important rival of the locally made Sharples Separator.

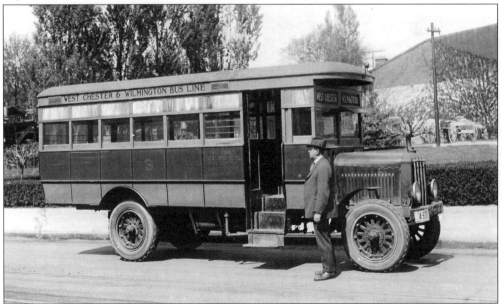

West Chester and the neighboring city of Wilmington were never connected by rail or trolley, but a bus line was established early between these two points. The West Chester and Wilmington Bus Company was later taken over by the Short Line Bus Company.

Caleb Taylor's general store was the oldest business in West Chester in 1899. This building, located south of Gay Street on Walnut Street, no longer stands.

This photograph shows a typical West Chester storefront. The display window contains small panes of glass and the narrow building's front door opens right on the street.

William Williams poses at his desk in Harry Taylor's real estate office on N. High Street in November 1916. Mr. Williams always sealed a real estate deal with a bit of whiskey. As evidenced by the almost empty bottle on his desk he was doing quite well. William R. Breuninger gave us this image of his great uncle.

Chain stores were in existence at the turn of the twentieth century. Daniel J. Karmerze, the local proprietor of the United Cigars Stores Co. at 16 W. Market Street, has decorated his store for the centennial of the borough. It appeared that a good 5¢ cigar could be bought in the borough in 1899.

By Earnest Request of Many of his Patients

HE IS WITH YOU AGAIN

FOR NINE DAYS.

THE GREATEST DISEASE DETECTIVE LIVING !

The Eyes of whom Disease Cannot Deceive.

Don't Miss the Only Chance You May Ever Have

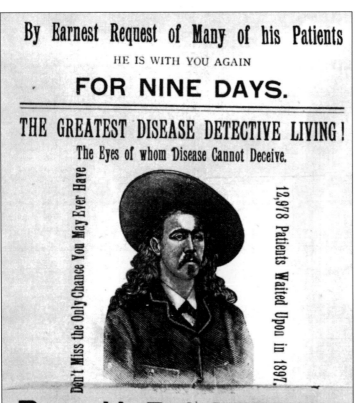

12,978 Patients Waited Upon in 1897.

PROF. H. P. LORMAN,

Better Known as the "INDIAN DOCTOR"

This is the man who has only to look at you and describe all your ailments—places his finger directly upon your pains and aches without feeling your pulse, looking at your tongue, or asking you any questions.

If you are doing well under the care of your family physician, and there is a reasonable prospect of recovery do not come to me.

Herbs, Roots, Barks, Gums and Balsams are the only remedies used by the Professor, and are furnished at his rooms.

CAN BE CONSULTED AT

EAGLE HOTEL, West Chester, Pa.,

From May 5th to 14th, 1898.

FREE OF CHARGE.

Hours: 9 to 12 A. M., 1 to 6 P. M. Evenings, 6.30 to 9. $1.00

ALL DAY SUNDAY I AM AT MY

HOME OFFICE, 1704 North Twentieth St., Phila.

☞ Come early and avoid the usual rush that are always waiting to see this wonderful Man. Children must be accompanied by a parent.

☞ Do not forget Prof. Lorman's Indian Oil for all pains and aches, or his death to worms, for grown up people as well as for children. His liver pills are unsurpassed. Oil, 25c., 50c., and $1.00. Worm powders, 50c. Liver pills, 25c. For sale at his office and at all druggists.

Professor H.P. Lorman, known as the "Indian doctor," traveled throughout the Philadelphia area. From March 5 to March 14 in 1899 he could be consulted at the Eagle Hotel at the northwest corner of Walnut and Gay Streets. Where is he today when we need him?

An important form of advertising from the Civil War to the early years of the twentieth century were trade cards like the one at right, distributed by George F. Brinton. Most businesses gave similar cards to their patrons, who often pasted them in scrapbooks.

GEO. F. BRINTON,
DEALER IN
Boots, Shoes, Trunks and Valises,
112 W. Gay St., West Chester, Pa.

Mayer and Eachus, located at 109 W. Market Street just beyond Church Street, was the leading sporting goods store at the turn of the nineteenth century. The rifles and handguns that they sold were marked with their own logo. Founded in 1882, they also made keys and provided for the hardware needs of the community for many years.

Thomas Stalker Butler was the U.S. Congressmen from this district from 1897 until his death in 1928. He served in the 55th Congress and the fifteen succeeding Congresses. He received two Japanese Cherry trees when they were originally planted at the Tidal Basin in Washington. He planted the trees at his home on W. Miner Street and one survives to this day. He was the father of General Smedley Darlington Butler and the grandfather of Thomas R. Butler, Esq.

Isabel Darlington was the first woman member of the Chester County Bar Association. She graduated from Wellesley in 1886 and was the second woman to receive her law degree from the University of Pennsylvania. She was the first and only woman lawyer in Chester County for almost fifty years. She is shown here at her desk in her law office at 16 E. Market Street. Her great nephew, Thomas R. Butler, still practices in this office.

Morris Cope was, among many things, a minister in the Society of Friends. He wrote *Some Authentic Extracts with a Few Deductions and Observations in Relation to the State of the Society of Friends*. This book was published by E.F. James in West Chester in 1858.

Chester County's foremost Realist artist was George Cope (1855–1929), a master of still life who was widely known as a painter of the Brandywine countryside. In 1894 he had a major commission to paint a picture of William F. Cody's equipment. Cody, or Buffalo Bill, was spending the winter in West Chester while his Wild West show was in winter quarters. Cope was often in need of money and would bring a painting into town in a basket and try to sell it. He is pictured here with his two grandsons.

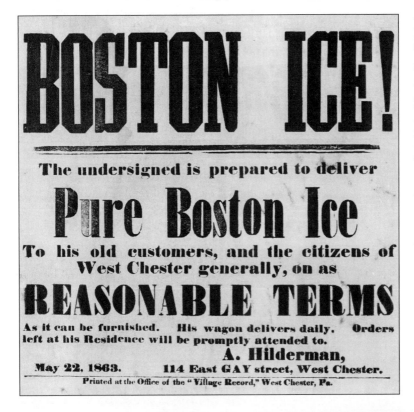

BOSTON ICE!

The undersigned is prepared to deliver

Pure Boston Ice

To his old customers, and the citizens of West Chester generally, on as

REASONABLE TERMS

As it can be furnished. His wagon delivers daily. Orders left at his Residence will be promptly attended to.

A. Hilderman,

May 22, 1863. 114 East GAY street, West Chester.

Printed at the Office of the "Village Record," West Chester, Pa.

By 1890 ice was produced locally by the West Chester Ice and Storage Company at the corner of Union and Franklin Street. Fred Heed was the superintendent and by 1899 5,000 tons of ice were being produced. In 1863, however, there was a need for imported ice as this broadside attests.

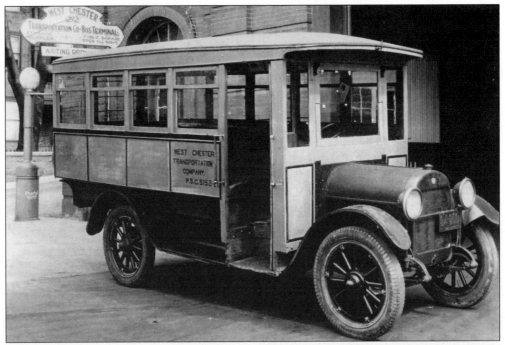

The above bus is an early example of bus transportation in the borough. The West Chester Transportation Company operated a terminal at 120 N. Walnut Street.

Charles W. Pennypacker was the Burgess of West Chester between the years 1903–1906. Pennypacker practiced law at his office at 13 N. High Street. He also wrote *The History of Downingtown, Pa.* in 1909, for their 50th anniversary celebration.

J. Warren Frame operated a grocery store on 118 E. Market Street, just east of the present M.S. Yearsleys. The building no longer stands.

George Fitzsimmons, a plumber and tin smith, poses at his store at 123 W. Market Street. He lived nearby at 102 W. Gay Street.

Five

Made in West Chester

In mild weather there is just enough for comfort. It responds to every change of weather conditions which makes it economical in fuel.

For particulars, address

Louis N. Davis

38 East Gay St.

West Chester, Pa.

FOR SALE BY

Davis Patent Regulating Valve

for

Vapor or Atmospheric System

of Heating

Louis N. Davis, Patentee

Office: 38 East Gay Street

West Chester, Pa.

Although there were several small industries in West Chester it was not considered a manufacturing town. Among the industries was a steam laundry, planing mill, tag factory, crayon factory, and a knitting factory. Louis Davis of 38 E. Gay Street invented and manufactured a regulating valve as shown by this pamphlet he used to advertise his product. Davis was a plumber, and gas and steam fitter, who specialized in heating by water and steam.

The Sharples Cream Separator Company was begun in West Chester in 1881 by P.M. Sharples. The first plant was on the southwest corner of Washington and Walnut Streets. The large factory complex on Patton Avenue was erected in 1889 and Sharples Separators were soon in general use throughout the United States. At the turn of the century it was the largest cream separator manufacturer in the country. Unfortunately the company was closed during the Depression.

The Sharples workers in this 1914 photograph are many of the people who are responsible for building West Chester. Can you find an ancestor in this group?

The Sharples Separator Company gave away many items to advertise their product. This song book appeared shortly after the turn of the century. By the start of the twentieth century Sharples was spending $20,000 a year on advertising alone. There were over 100 salesmen traveling in the U.S., Europe, and Africa. There were several branch offices in the U.S. and one in Australia.

This view of the Schramm Air Compressor at work in a quarry was an advertisement given away about 1918.

The Hoopes Bros. and Darlington Wheel Works was begun in 1866 by William and Thomas Hoopes at their farm one mile northwest of town. The spokes were made of Chester County hickory and oak timber after proper drying and fitting of the material. The wheel works moved to West Chester in 1867 to the corner of E. Market Street and the Pennsylvania Railroad, as shown in this picture. The third partner was Edward S. Darlington. (Photograph courtesy of The Delaware Agricultural Museum and Village.)

By the turn of the century the wheel works employed approximately 225 men, most of whom were from West Chester, and produced about 35,000 sets per year. The quality of wheels produced was renowned throughout the U.S. This image shows the proud workers at the wheel works about 1905. (Photograph courtesy of The Delaware Agricultural Museum and Village.)

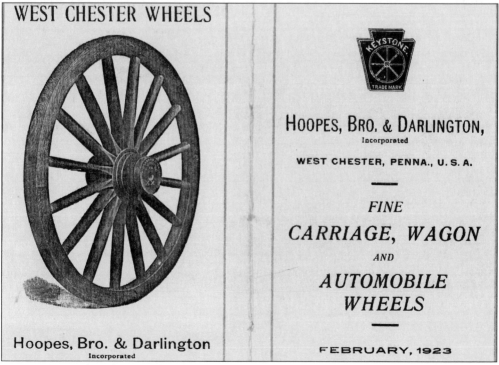

Hoopes Bro. and Darlington also made baseball bats and skis. The chief builders of fire engines in the country bought from the West Chester company as well as the person who was known to produce the best buggies in the country. The same care was used to make the four qualities of wheels; only the quality of the timber used was different.

This advertisement for the wheel works appeared around the turn of the century.

The Keystone Gasoline Engine was manufactured in West Chester by the Rothwell Manufacturing Company. The engines were produced in the second decade of the twentieth century.

Among products produced by Frederick Darlington on N. Walnut Street was the Aquarium Fountain.

In the later half of the nineteenth century West Chester was a center for the nursery business. Among the many nurseries were the Morris Nursery, established in 1849, J. Lacey Darlington and Company, and Otto and Achelis. Achelis had 2,000 acres of ground under cultivation and 200 square feet under glass. Hoopes, Bro. and Thomas was established in 1853 and was one of the largest nurseries in the United States. The Morris Nursery Co. sold the Catalpa Bungei, the unusual ornamental plant shown here.

John Hall was a watch and clockmaker who worked in West Chester in the middle of the nineteenth century. The sun dial on the Chester County Court House lawn was made by Hall. This is an example of a watch paper placed in a watch repaired by this well-respected craftsman.

Six

Desks, Pews, and Benches

West Chester schools were first opened in the spring of 1837 and by 1839 there were nine schools and nine teachers. West Chester High School, which graduated its first class in 1866, occupied this building from 1863 until 1906. The building was razed during World War I and many of the bricks were re-used in the Biddle Street School, which was an elementary school. The new West Chester High School, built in 1906 and destroyed by fire in 1947, is shown on the right.

The Gay Street Public School was built in 1895 from the design of West Chester native Arthur Ebbs Willauer for African-Americans students. This building was destroyed by fire in 1908. A new school was built and was integrated in 1957. A new Borough Hall replaced the school in the 1990s. (Photograph courtesy of the Chester County Historical Society.)

Warren Burton, far right in the last row, coached this football team at the Gay Street School. Burton graduated from West Chester High School in 1923 and became a prominent local educator.

The Barnard Street School, built in 1841, was the first public school erected in West Chester. The cost of the school was $2,900. Prior to that time classes were held in churches, the post office, and meetinghouses. The school was open from 8 am to noon and from 2 pm until 5 pm. The primary grades were on the first floor and the secondary grades were on the second floor. The secondary grades moved to the Church Street building four years later. (Photograph courtesy of the Chester County Historical Society.)

Designed by T. Roney Williamson, the High Street School was built in 1889. It served as an elementary school for the residents of the southern half of the borough. The school was built on part of the original Sharples homestead. It was razed in 1978.

Elmira H. Lincoln Phelps established a young ladies seminary in 1837. To house this school she hired Thomas U. Walter to design a state-of-the-art building. The train in the foreground is an anachronism as in 1837 the railroad was pulled by horses. The school failed and the building was sold at a sheriff's sale to Antoine Brunin de Bolmar, a native of France. Bolmar, known as the "Napoleon of teachers," ran a boys school there from 1840 to 1860.

The center part of Villa Maria is the old Phelps seminary. The Pennsylvania Military Institute used the facility from 1862 to 1865. The military institute moved to Chester, Pa., in 1865, and the school later became Widener College.

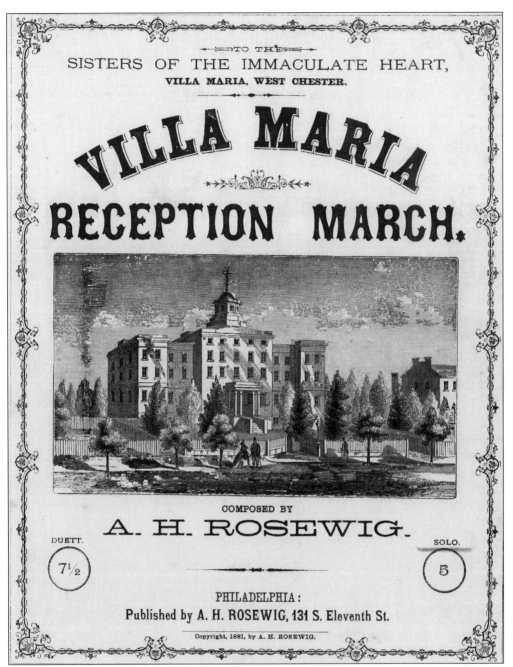

The Sisters of the Immaculate Heart operated a girls school, Villa Maria, on this site from 1873 until the 1960s, when they moved to nearby Immaculata College. An apartment complex is now located on this property.

CATALOGUE

OF THE

OFFICERS AND STUDENTS

OF THE

WEST CHESTER ACADEMY

FOR YOUNG MEN AND BOYS,

WEST CHESTER, PENN'A.

1867-68.

~~~~~~~~~~

WEST CHESTER:
REPUBLICAN, BOOK, CARD AND JOB PRINTER.
1868.

This is the catalogue of the West Chester Academy on W. Gay Street. West Chester was known as the "Athens of Pennsylvania," not only because of the many fine examples of Greek Revival architecture, but also because of the numerous and excellent private schools located here. Dr. George Smith, author of *The History of Delaware County*, James B. Everhart, Joseph Hemphill, and William W. Jefferis, were among the academy graduates.

74

The Darlington Seminary on W. Miner Street beyond the edge of the borough was operated by Richard Darlington. This prominent girls school, begun here in 1883, existed for over fifty years. The original school was located at Ercildoun, near Coatesville, but was destroyed by a tornado in 1877.

The Darlington Seminary was the first trolley stop west of the borough on the way to Lenape. The trolley stop is still there today. This photograph of a May pole dance on the playground shows another home, Round Top, in the distance.

The original barn on the Ingram farm, a Chester County bank barn, was made into a natatorium for the Darlington Seminary.

Price's Boarding School was built by Nathan H. Sharples in 1829 on Union Street west of High. Sharples' in-laws, Philip and Rachel Price, ran the school with their daughter until 1852 as a Friend's coeducational school. The McClellan Institute, shown here, occupied the building from 1871 to 1875. How many students can you find in the picture?

Although the community was largely settled by Friends, at the beginning of the twentieth century there were fifteen organizations representing seven different denominations with their branches. The Jordan Tabernacle was built on the site of the present armory on N. High Street. In the second decade of the this century revivals were held here by the various protestant churches. The picture below shows the interior of the Jordan Tabernacle.

The Westminster Presbyterian Church was designed by Arthur Stanley Cochran. Cochran, a member of the church, died January on 1, 1899, and did not live to see the church completed. It was built of Avondale stone in the Gothic style at a cost of approximately $18,000. The church was completed in 1899 for the centennial of West Chester. It is currently the home of the Emmanuel Baptist Church. The bell tree, a weeping beech, is still a local landmark.

The Olivet Baptist Church at S. New and Union Streets, designed by Professor Joseph J. Baily, was built of blue limestone. The church was organized at the Opera House in April 1897. The membership totaled 118, all but one of whom had been members of the First Baptist Church. The Reformed Presbyterian Church now occupies the building.

The Methodist church, designed by Thomas U. Walter, was erected at the corner of Darlington and Market Streets in 1842. To raise the money for the church a system of rented pews was adopted. This system was abolished in 1851.

Richard Newton, formerly a pastor of The Holy Trinity Episcopal Church, founded The Church of the Sure Foundation (Reformed Episcopal) in 1884 with seventeen charter members. The followers refused to be bound by the restrictions of the High Church Episcopalians. The first services were held in the old Holy Trinity Protestant Episcopal Church on W. Gay Street. The Church of the Sure Foundation's new sanctuary was attached to the east end of Price's Boarding School on W. Union Street, c. 1906.

The First Presbyterian Church, also designed by Thomas U. Walter, is located at 130 W. Miner Street. Completed in 1834, it is the oldest extant church structure in the borough. Fifty-one charter members held meetings in the courthouse before moving into the church. Rev. William A. Stevens, who was instrumental in organizing the church, was the first minister. Sadly, he died at the age of twenty-eight, one year after the church was organized. The Sunday school addition on the left was designed by T. Roney Williamson in 1893. Who else?

This calendar photograph shows the first Salvation Army officer and his family to serve in West Chester.

Christ's Church was the first place of worship in West Chester. This small one-story brick structure was erected in 1793 on the north side of W. Gay Street. St. Agnes was built during the administration of Father John F. Prendergast for the cost of $6,000 to accommodate the growing congregation. The cornerstone-laying ceremony was held on September 29, 1852, before a large gathering of borough residents. The building was replaced by the present church in 1926.

The Holy Trinity Episcopal Church moved to S. High Street from its original Gay Street location in 1868. Construction of this serpentine church was completed in 1892. The tower, designed by T. Roney Williamson, has since been taken down because the serpentine stone was weakened from the weather.

This very early photograph shows the High Street Friends Meeting House before the new brick meetinghouse was built. The serpentine stone structure was completed in 1813, the eastern half of which survives as the social room in the current meetinghouse. Isaac Sharples was the first clerk and elders included familiar names such as Cope, Price, and Jefferis. Also in this picture is the High Street Friends School, built in 1860 at a cost of $1,210.80.

The Chestnut Street Meeting House, built by the Orthodox or Arch Street Friends in 1844, was constructed of serpentine. At the time of the centennial the meeting had 135 members. When the High and Chestnut Street Meetings were re-united in the 1950s this building was used by the West Chester Day Care Center. The building was torn down in 1967 for a municipal parking lot.

Seven

The Normal

On May 24, 1870, a resolution to build the Normal School was adopted at the Chester County Court House. By 1888 the State Normal School for the First District of Pennsylvania, which included Chester, Bucks, Montgomery, and Delaware Counties, consisted of a massive four-story serpentine building and 10 acres of property. Shown here are Dr. George Morris Philips, principal, with his wife, Elizabeth M. Philips, and their bulldog Puck on the front porch of Green Gables. Puck was the school's mascot but lost a battle with a street car on August 5, 1904. His most untimely death was noted with much sadness.

During the early years the Normal School was in the countryside south of town. This view in 1882 shows the main building and the infirmary boiler room, which were later connected and became the largest serpentine stone building in the country.

This building, which became known as "Old Main," was designed by Addison Hutton. The center section was completed in 1871. The north and south wings were completed by 1883. The building was razed in the 1970s .

Two young college students pose in their dorm room on the third floor of Old Main during the early part of the twentieth century.

Green Gables, the principal's home on the southwest corner of Normal Avenue and High Street, was built in 1891 during George M. Philips' tenure. The Philips were the only family to occupy this residence. T. Roney Williamson designed the house, which cost $12,333.46 to build. Green Gables was demolished to build Philips Memorial Hall.

The Infirmary or Sanitarium, located on Rosedale Avenue east of High Street, was erected in 1892. The building in the distance is the center part of Tanglewood, the residence of the university president.

The new gymnasium that was built in 1889 was the second largest gym in the nation at that time. The plan by T. Roney Williamson was based on Hemenway Gym at Harvard. The total cost was $27,545.84. To the left and rear of the gym is Recitation Hall, also constructed of serpentine stone.

The main gymnasium floor was 100 feet long by 50 feet wide. Twelve feet above the floor was a running track, twenty laps to the mile. This exercise class in 1916 is thought to be the first co-educational gym class at the Normal.

George M. Philips and the faculty of the Normal pose on the steps in front of the library, c. 1910.

The Class of 1907 presents their junior class play in the chapel in Old Main. The Della Robbia panels were given to the Normal School as a class gift.

A meeting of the staff of the senior publication, *The Serpentine*, was held in a reading room in the library, *c.* 1917. *The Serpentine* was first published in 1912.

Members of the Class of 1912 pose on the steps of the library along with their class banner. Each class chose their own colors and banner.

These Normal School students are taking their teacher certification examinations in the large third-floor classroom in Old Main, *c.* 1893.

George Morris Philips, principal of the Normal from 1881 until his death in 1920, poses at his desk in his office at Green Gables. During his tenure the gymnasium, Recitation Hall, Green Gables, the Model School, the library, the Infirmary, and Wayne Hall were added to the campus.

The 1916 football team is shown here on the athletic field. From left to right in the background are Recitation Hall, the library, and Wayne Hall.

Students in front of Old Main on S. High Street gather to welcome the football team home from Shippensburg College.

The Demonstration School, now known as Ruby Jones Hall on the campus of West Chester University, was erected as the Model School for West Chester Normal School in 1899. Students from the Normal School, as part of their course work, could view master teachers as they taught their students in K-6 classrooms.

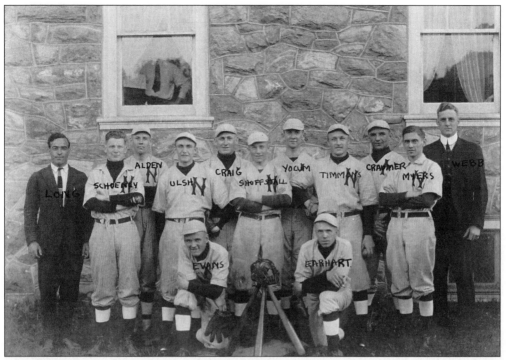

Many of the names of the members of the 1914 baseball team are still familiar in and around West Chester. The photograph was taken in front of Wayne Hall.

The Normal was renowned for its athletic and music programs. The State Normal School Band is shown here seated on the steps of the gym in 1910.

The YMCA, an organization for young men, was formed in October 1890. The young men vowed to treat all women with respect and endeavored to protect them from wrong and degradation. Frances Harvey Green and the officers of the YMCA are seated on the steps of Green's house on the corner of Linden and Walnut Streets.

The 1916 varsity lettermen are sitting on the library steps for their yearbook picture.

Women sports at the Normal were important early on as part of their overall education. These five players of the 1904 basketball team are posing in the gymnasium.

The Student Army Training Corps (SATC) is shown here in 1918. Wayne Field served as the training camp for the military corps, consisting of 110 students divided into three age groups. Students lived under military discipline in Wayne Hall and attended special classes. One hundred and eight SATC graduates served in World War I.

The athletic fields were once the Chester County Agricultural Society fairgrounds. The grandstand was built in 1900 at the cost of $4,785.04. It was destroyed by fire fifty years later. The small ticket office on the west side of the stands was moved to the Bull Center parking lot where it remains.

In 1915 the Normal purchased 10.5 acres adjacent to the infirmary on Rosedale Avenue. Arthur Cromwell, professor of Agriculture, rented the farm and used the grounds as a farm laboratory for his students. It was often referred to as "the pig farm." The above barn is now the garage at Tanglewood.

Attending daily chapel was compulsory during Dr. Philips' tenure. The chapel was located in "Old Main." This picture by C.S. Bradford was taken in 1887.

Eight

Idle Hours

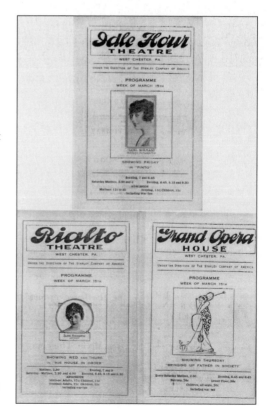

The Brandywine Baseball Club, the West Chester Gun Club, the West Chester Cricket Club, the West Chester Tennis Club, and the West Chester Roque Club, were among the many athletic clubs people joined at the turn of the century. The social and political clubs included the West Chester Pioneer Corp #1, the Chester County Republican Club, the West Chester Club, the Bachelors Club, the Home Cluster, and the Male Quartet. Marshall Square Park and Brandywine Creek were also a major source of recreation and enjoyment.

West Chester boasted of three movie theaters at the time this advertisement appeared. The Rialto and Idle Hour were on the first block of E. Gay Street. The Grand Opera House was on N. High Street just above the Chester County Court House. The Court House Annex is on that site today.

There were numerous baseball clubs in the area during this period. The Gay Street Baseball Club played on Sharples Field on the northeast corner of Penn and Gay Streets. Alger Whitcraft Sr. is in the center of this *c.* 1900 photograph with his arms folded. The Gay Street Plaza has since been built on the field.

The Brandywine Baseball Club played on the Normal School field. In the background is the Model School and Recitation Hall, *c.* 1900.

The George A. McCall Post of the Grand Army of the Republic was given the Horticultural Hall as a meeting place by Uriah Hunt Painter. There was a proviso that when the last surviving member of the Post died the building would be turned over to the Chester County Historical Society. Members of the Post are shown here standing in front of that building, *c.* 1915.

Picnicking and canoeing on the Brandywine was a favorite summer pastime. There were seasonal cottages for local residents who would spend the weekend and summer vacations by the creek. The Brandywine was a very popular place for many of the clubs, societies, and athletic groups to spend their leisure time.

Ann Eliza Hastings, the oldest resident of West Chester, is shown here in 1919. She was born on March 25, 1813, in Framingham, Massachusetts. She was 106 when this portrait of her was taken.

At a meeting of the Chester County Historical Society on February 20, 1919, George Morris Philips gave an account of twenty-one citizens of West Chester then living who were more than ninety years of age. These nine residents were among that group. From left to right are as follows: (front row) Mary Eachus, 92; Caroline Hoopes Garrett, 92; Dr. Jesse C. Green, 102; Elizabeth Pierce Yerkes, 100; Elizabeth P. Broomall, 91; and Sarah Howard Davis, 92; (back row) John Ralston, 92; James McElree, 94; and Thomas A. Blanken, 94.

The Normal School added greatly to the cultural life of the area. Many musical and dramatic programs were presented by the students. This program was for a musical recital of the Class of 1899, held on June 25 at 8 pm. "Doing, not dreaming, is the secret of success."

Junior Recital,

Class of
Ninety-nine,

State Normal School,
West Chester, Pa.

Saturday,
June 25, 1898,

At 8 O'clock.

"Doing, not dreaming, is the secret of success."

The new Borough hall was dedicated on March 10, 1912. The above group attended the dedication and dinner. The building now houses a restaurant and is located a few doors south of Market Street on High.

The centennial celebration of the founding of West Chester was held in October of 1899. October 11 was Educational Day, October 12 was Civic Day, and October 13 was Fireman's Day. This arch is located in front of the First West Chester Fire Company building on N. Church Street. The First West Chester Fire Company was also celebrating its' 100th anniversary.

Fred Heed was a member of Borough Council and the chairman of the decorating committee for the centennial. Fred and Edith Heed and their nine children lived in this home on the southwest corner of Gay and Darlington Streets.

Merchants took the opportunity to decorate their stores for the celebration. The business on the far right was Beatty and Son, Tailors. This building was later the site of Mosteller's Store on W. Gay Street and is now part of the Chester County Court House Annex.

The Anne Y. Stone dwelling on the northeast corner of Market and Walnut Streets is a fine example of the enthusiasm of borough residents in their support of the centennial.

This photograph shows the major intersection, High and Gay Streets, on the day of one of the parades for the centennial celebration. On October 12 the Civic Day parade included military and civic organizations, and a display of floats. The Fireman's parade on October 13 included demonstrations by the firemen and invited guests.

The West Chester Lyceum, a literary society founded by people interested in lectures, discussions, and concerts, also enjoyed picnics and outside entertainment. This gathering of the Lyceum in July 1897 was held at Indian Deep on the western branch of the Brandywine Creek above Northbrook.

In the summertime life was often more relaxed particularly for people living in the countryside. There were more opportunities for family pictures and it was a special occasion to have a photographer take pictures such as this one at the Mellor Farm. The farm, located on Strasburg Road west of the borough, was the birthplace of Gilbert Cope.

Gilbert and Anna Garrett Cope and their three children, Herman, Joseph, and Ellen, pose in their garden at 532 N. Church Street. Gilbert Cope was born on August 17, 1840, at the family homestead on Strasburg Road near the Black Horse Tavern. Gilbert Cope was the youngest of the eight children of Joseph and Eliza Gilbert Cope. He worked his entire life on Chester County genealogy and history. He is considered the best known county historian with the publication of *Chester County History* and twelve other major works.

Balloon ascensions were popular public attractions at the turn of the century. Most of the rides were taken in a tethered balloon, however.

Many groups owned cabins along the Brandywine Creek at Lenape to use for outside activities. The West Chester Athletic Club is shown here in front of their bungalow in November 1912. Those present include William Wetherill, J. Walter Keech, Wilmer T. Lewis, William Mullin, Edward G. Hoopes, Fred F. Hickman, J.D. Harris, Edwin S. Turner, Edward J. Dawson, Warren T. Garrett, Glen W. Hall, Joseph Hampton, Harry Peoples, and William Patton, cook.

The Pennsylvania State Grange held their meeting in West Chester on December 12, 1907. Their banquet for nearly 1,000 people was held in the Sharples Separator Factory in their new building before the machinery was installed.

The West Chester Rotary Club gathered on the Normal School campus in front of Recitation Hall in July 1922, after a baseball game with the Chester Rotary Club. West Chester Rotary was started in 1921 and celebrated seventy-five years of service in 1996.

Alfred Sharples is shown here working in his garden at 22 Dean Street at the turn of the century.

William Lynch, proprietor of the West Chester Hotel, with this broadside announced that the three largest pigs would be slaughtered at his hotel on January 30, 1865.

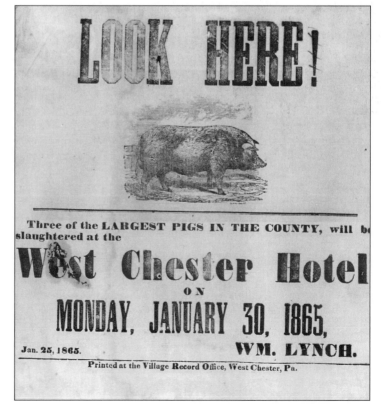

This crowd gathered on June 11, 1915, for the dedication of Chester County's monument to those who served in the Union Army from the area.

The Marine Band in West Chester gave a public concert at the Sharples Park on the corner of Gay and Penn Streets after the dedication ceremony of "Old Glory" on June 11, 1915.

Nine

Close to Home

The second post office to be established in Chester County was in West Chester. For many years the job of postmaster was a part-time job because of lack of business. In 1899 there were twenty-seven in-bound and twenty-four out-bound mails daily. Beginning in 1899, mail was delivered to residents free of charge. Free rural delivery was also begun in 1899. The rural routes extended 4 to 6 miles in each direction.

Within 2 miles of West Chester is the Brandywine Creek and the beautiful rolling hills of Chester County. The area surrounding the borough is also rich in historic battlefields such as Brandywine, Birmingham, Chadds Ford, Paoli, and the encampment at Valley Forge.

Sconneltown, a country crossroads 1.5 miles west of the borough, rivaled West Chester in size during the colonial period. The above view was taken one block east of Sconneltown on Birmingham Road where the trolley from West Chester to Lenape crossed. The sign on the oak tree states that General Howe and the British Army reached this spot in the early afternoon of September 11, 1777, while on his way to the Brandywine Battle. The Birmingham Friends had moved their benches to a blacksmith shop here and were holding their meeting. Their meetinghouse had been taken over by the Americans for use as a hospital.

W. Miner Street at the western edge of the borough appears rural in this postcard, c. 1906. The frame buildings on the right are part of Everhart's grove. The stone building on the left is Old Zion, founded by an African-American congregation. It was dedicated in 1838 and was used until the Civil War. The area in the vicinity of the church was settled by the African-American residents of West Chester. The church moved to a schoolhouse on the corner of Barnard and Adams Street. It eventually became Bethel A.M.E.

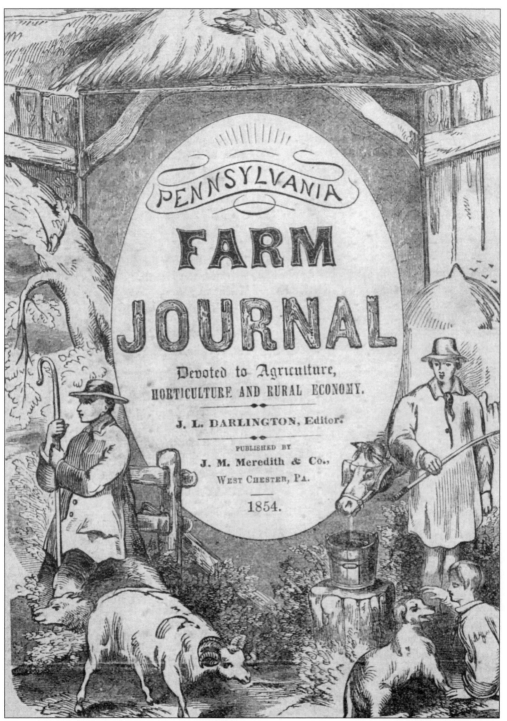

The first volume of *The Pennsylvania Farm Journal* was printed in Lancaster, PA. *The Journal* was moved to West Chester in 1852 by J. Lacey Darlington, the son of Dr. William Darlington. Darlington operated the Agricultural Warehouse at the southeast corner of Chestnut and High Streets. *The Journal* later moved to Philadelphia.

The Octagonal Schoolhouse at Birmingham was built in 1819. The eight-sided building housed eight separate grades. Originally a Friend's school, it was later used by the public school system for many years. This old structure was the polling place for Birmingham Township until recent years.

At one time there were close to one hundred covered bridges in Chester County. Jefferis Bridge was built in 1833 where W. Miner Street crossed the Brandywine Creek. It was destroyed by fire in 1953. On September 11, 1777, the British Army crossed the creek at Jefferis Ford, where the bridge was later built, on the way to the Battle of Brandywine.

The construction of Greystone, the palatial estate of P.M. Sharples, was begun in 1905 and completed in 1907. It was created as a modern version of an English Jacobean country house. The mansion, lakes, ponds, gardens, and fields covered approximately 700 acres.

Daniel Hoopes purchased the northwest quadrant of West Chester on June 6, 1728. The parcel of land extended from Gay Street to St. Agnes Cemetery on the west side of High Street. The land was originally patented to Nathanial Puckle in 1701 from William Penn. Hoopes divided the 630 acres among his children. His son Nathan built the Taylor Mill House, above, which still stands.

Thomas Hoopes built this house in 1739. In 1866 the Hoopes Brothers and Darlington Wheel Works began operation on this property. On the front lawn the path is paved with mill stones once used in a local gristmill. During the Civil War the Hoopes barn was burned by Southern sympathizers. The house was named Madryn by Anna D. Embree after her home in Wales.

Lenape Park was established by the West Chester Street Railway as a method of increasing ridership. For many years the last stop was at Lenape Park. It was later extended to West Grove, PA., via Kennett Square. The building is the canoe house which is used today as the studio of artist Tom Bostelle. The postcard shown here was used as a dance card for the young ladies who attended dances held at the park. You could sign up for the two step, one step, waltz, hesitation, tango, or the prize waltz.

Another branch of the Hoopes family built this stone dwelling in East Bradford Township, along Copeland School Road. This house was built in two sections. The original part of the house was built in the first half of the nineteenth century. Note the two date stones on the front of the house.

FOR SALE.

A VALUABLE plantation ſituate in the townſhip of Goſhen in the county of Cheſter, and ſtate of Pennſylvania. Containing 36 acres, 7 of which are good meadow with about 5 acres of wood land, and a good orchard of variouſly grafted fruit trees. On the premiſes are erected a commodious two ſtory ſtone dwelling houſe, with a log barn, and ſtables under ... For terms apply to the ſubſcriber living at the houſe of James Hemphill.

HENRY GUEST.

January the 9th, 1798.

This is the oldest known surviving broadside printed in Chester County. The firm of Jones, Hoff, and Derrick, removed from Philadelphia to West Chester in 1794, to escape the Yellow Fever epidemic. This firm printed the newspaper which serves as the frontispiece for this book. That newspaper is the first piece of printing done in Chester County. Philip Derrick, one of the partners, remained in West Chester and married the daughter of the first Burgess, William Sharples. He continued his trade in West Chester into the nineteenth century.

Gilbert Cope took this picture of the Birmingham Friends Meeting House sometime before the turn of the twentieth century. This historic building was used as a hospital by both the American and the British armies at the time of the Battle of Brandywine. The left section, centered on the door, was erected in 1763 and was extended to the right in 1818. Today Birmingham Meeting stands in a beautiful grove of trees.

This Quaker elementary school was built by Birmingham Orthodox Friends in the 1854. The structure was raised to two stories and serves as a residence today.

Oaklands cemetery covers 26 acres north of the borough on Pottstown Pike. The chapel in this *c.* 1900 photograph was located in the center of the cemetery. Many prominent residents of the area are buried here.

Strode's Mill, named after the Strode family, is on the busy corner of the Lenape and Birmingham Roads. It is no longer the quiet rural crossroads appears here in 1890. This mill ground flour for area farmers for decades.

The home on the left was built before the Revolution on the east side of Jefferis Ford on the Brandywine Creek. It was the residence of the James family for many years. About the turn of the century Edwin James built the mansion on the right and was in the process of tearing down the old homestead when this picture was taken. The mansion stands on the corner of W. Miner Street and Creek Road.

Oermead Farm just west of the borough on Strasburg Road was the country farmstead of the Howell family. Joshua Howell owned this property when this photograph was taken, c. 1890. Howell's daughter Deborah married Francis Brinton and together they ran an antique business for over sixty years. About 1910 Deborah Brinton walked to the bottom of the field behind her house and boarded a trolley to West Chester and continued her trip to Boston by the various connecting trolley lines.

The main building of Westtown School, built in 1888, used the design of Addison Hutton. This Quaker co-educational boarding school was founded in 1799. Westtown School celebrates its bicentennial the same year at the borough of West Chester, 1999.

Cope's bridge was built in 1807 where the Strasburg Road crosses the eastern branch of the Brandywine River. The Cope Iron Factory is visible through the archway of the bridge.

The Grove Methodist Church, the earliest Methodist church in Chester County, was founded in 1774. At the turn of the century this was considered to be in the country. The second Burgess of West Chester, Jacob Ehrenzellar, and Thomas Ogden, cabinetmaker, are buried in the graveyard next to the church. The tree to the far left of the church is a black oak nearly 300 years old. It was alive when William Penn came to Pennsylvania in 1682 and still survives.

These stone gate posts mark the entrance on Cemetery Hill to the Orthodox Friends burial grounds. An ordinance was passed in 1852 that prohibited burial grounds within the borough limits. The Friends closed their burial ground on the southeast corner of Gay and Bradford Avenues and moved the graves to this site. Among the noteworthy Friends buried here are George and Gilbert Cope, Arthur James, and Isaac Israel Hayes, the Arctic explorer.

Brooznoll, built by Daniel Hoopes in 1723, was located along Street Road east of Tanguy. Hoopes later moved to the borough as one of its earlier settlers.

This house was located on the dirt road that connected Lenape Road with Sconneltown Road following the trolley route. It was the home of Willis P. Hazzard, historian, dairyman, and ornithologist, who amassed a large and valuable collection of early documents, records, and books. He wrote the third volume of *Watson's Annals of Philadelphia*, a book of judging prize cattle, and a genealogy of the Pennsylvania Hazzard family. Hazzard lived at Maple Knoll from 1865 until it was destroyed by fire in 1904 along with all of the priceless collections. Hazzard died in 1910.

Thornbury Cottage stands on Street Road one block east of Westtown Station. The railroad bridge can be seen on the right in this photograph taken *c*. 1904. This house is hidden from view by a fence and shrubbery.

This dirt road leaving West Chester on the way to Wilmington, Delaware, is now U.S. Route 202.

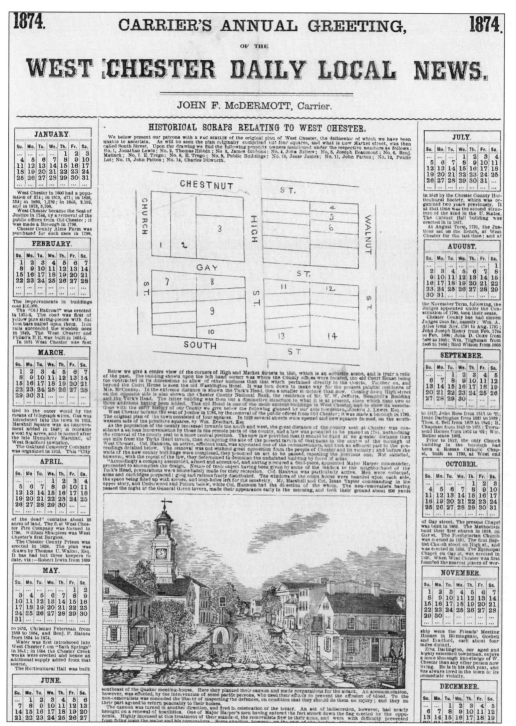

Before Christmas, during the nineteenth century, paper boys would distribute a calendar for the coming year to their patrons, thus reminding them of their past service and secretly hoping to be remembered by a small gift. This *Daily Local News* annual greeting shared the early history of the borough and reproduced the Sherman Day woodcut looking north on High Street.

Acknowledgments

Without the generosity of many people we would not have been able to complete this book. The following either loaned photographs, shared memories, or gave us technical assistance:

Leslee G. Petrondi, Larry McDevitt, Betsy and Ted Lawrence, Thomas R. Butler, Esq., William Supplee, John Supplee, James A. Whitcraft, Ashton B.T. Smith Jr., Dr. Edmundo Morales, Liz Heed, Dr. Marshall Becker, Caroline Rubincam, Alger Whitcraft, Tyson Cooper, Bill and Shirley Breuninger, Bill Anderson, Phillip Neff, III, Louise Darlington, Linda Mahan, Reese Mahan, Florence Miller, Dr. Russell L. Sturzebecker, Joan Osborne, Trudy Allen, Jack Webster, Gerald Schoelkopf, Jerry Williams, West Chester University, and the Delaware Agriculture and Farm Museum.

A special note of thanks to my two soul mates, Marty Grover and Madeleine Wing Adler, for their encouragement and sense of humor. Lastly to my two favorite future historians, Jaime and Joshua, for making projects such as this more meaningful.